MW01154031

THE NEW
JERSEY SHORE
Dictionary

Published by DS Publications, East Berlin, CT

Printed in the United States of America

Library of Congress Cataloging-in-Publication Data

ISBN 978-1-456-34708-6

First Edition

THE NEW JERSEY SHORE

Dictionary

DISCLAIMER

**THIS IS AN ADULT OVER 18
PARODY BOOK.**

**IF YOU ARE OFFENDED BY ADULT
OR PARODY MATERIAL
PLEASE DO NOT READ
ANY FURTHER
AND DISPOSE
OF THE BOOK PROPERLY.**

RATING SYSTEM 1-10
6-10 = HOTTIE -OR- GORILLA
4-5 = LANDMINE
2-3 = GRENADE
1 = BOTTOM OF THE BARREL

SPECIAL CATEGORIES
HI = HIPPOPATUMUS
J = JUICEHEAD
TR = TRENADE

LITTLE BLACK BOOK DIGITZ

GUIDO/GUIDETTE	DIGITZ	RATING

LITTLE BLACK BOOK DIGITZ

GUIDO/GUIDETTE	DIGITZ	RATING
_____	_____	_____
_____	_____	_____
_____	_____	_____
_____	_____	_____
_____	_____	_____
_____	_____	_____
_____	_____	_____
_____	_____	_____
_____	_____	_____
_____	_____	_____
_____	_____	_____
_____	_____	_____
_____	_____	_____
_____	_____	_____
_____	_____	_____

LITTLE BLACK BOOK DIGITZ

GUIDO/GUIDETTE	DIGITZ	RATING
_____	_____	_____
_____	_____	_____
_____	_____	_____
_____	_____	_____
_____	_____	_____
_____	_____	_____
_____	_____	_____
_____	_____	_____
_____	_____	_____
_____	_____	_____
_____	_____	_____
_____	_____	_____
_____	_____	_____
_____	_____	_____

CONTENTS

INDEX   I

ATOMIC BOMB
Pronounced: (a-tom-ik bom)
Adjective,Noun
Really Really fugly Girl. Used by members of the MVP to describe certain club goers.
Adjective
"Those two girls are two solid 'atomic bomb' bitches."
Noun
"Jill and Vanessa are two solid atomic bombs!"
See also **Fugly**, **Grenade**, **Tank**, **Landmine**.

ALL IN
Pronounced: (ahll inn)
_Expression
Means at the casino. Can be any casino.
Also means lets go together, everyone will be going out.
"We are all in for going to the beach!"

BANGIN

Pronounced: (bayngin)
Adjective
Describing how hot a woman is. Usually in reference to looks or body.
"Those girls from the club were bangin'!"
See also **Hot**.

BATTLE

Pronounced: (batl)
Verb
To dance in a competitive manner in a club as house music plays loudly.
"Let's go Vin, time to battle on the floor!"

BEATIN UP THE BEAT

Phrase
This phrase is used when you are in a club and the music is pounding and loud. The loud music causes you to pound the ground with your fists. As you are pounding the ground and the music builds you start rising from the floor and eventually stand. The next step is to transfer to a fist pump.
See also **Fist Pump**.

BLOCK ROCKER

Pronounced: (block rock-er)
Adjective, Noun
Description of a large (i.e. fat) woman.
Adjective
"Did you see that block rockin' chick by the bar ?"
Noun
"Sandy is a block rocker!"
See also **Rugged**.

BLOWOUT

Pronounced: (bloaut)
Noun
A hairstyle that is faded from skin to about ½ inch in length from the edge of the hairline up an inch. The rest of the hair is left the same length, 1-2 inches. Next the hair is spiked up in chunks with heavy use of gel or mousse.
Also called a 'Brooklyn Fade', 'Brooklyn', 'temp' or a 'tape up'.

Origin
The origin of the blowout is debated, some believe a Brooklyn barbershop started the trend but many in the Northeast say it started at a barbershop in Berlin, CT. The trend appeared in the Northeast, particularly in Philadelphia, parts of New York and New Jersey.

Current Use
There are also blowout parties, pub-crawls, and viewing parties which feature the hairstyle.
"Hey Bro! Check out the blowout!
See also **Pouf**.

BOLT-ONS

Pronounced: (bolt-awns)

Noun

Term used for breast implants.

"Check out the <u>bolt-ons</u> she's sportin'. She's got me chubbed up six ways to Sunday."

See also **Ta-Ta's**.

BOUNCE

Pronounced: (bawn ss)

Verb

Describes the act of leaving a location. Also refers to leaving before you do something stupid.

"This club is lame let's bounce."

"Let's bounce before I get into trouble."

BOTTOM LINE

Pronounced: (bot-tum lyne)

Phrase

The point or topic of the discussion.

"<u>Bottom line</u> is you're getting naked and we are going to smoosh."

BOTTOM OF THE BARREL

Pronounced: (bot-tum of the bare-rel)
Phrase
Used to exaggerate something being said.
"Those girls last night were <u>bottom of the barrel</u>."
See also **Landmine, Grenade**

BRO

Pronounced: (brro)
Noun
A male best friend.
"Hey Bro! Can't wait to hit the club tonight!
See also **Bro-Code.**

BRO-CODE

Pronounced: (brro ko-d)
Noun
A set of rules meant to be a guideline to live by between best friends (Bro's) . The Bro Code can also include punishments for breaking these rules and laws. The rules must be followed if you wish to remain friends. The rules began as unwritten rules to follow, but because of the Pussification of America, haven't been followed properly and for some men they needed to be spelled out in bold print.
"I can't believe it! Kurt isn't following the bro-code! I never thought his arrogant ass would do that!"
See also **Bro, Pussification.**

BROMANCE

Pronounced: (brro mans)

Noun

A close but non-sexual relationship between two (or more) men, a form of homosocial intimacy. It describes two guys that really like each other a lot. They may spend a lot of time together. They are heterosexual. Bromance is a combination of two words – brother and romance.

Friendships are primarily based on shared activities, instead of emotional sharing (which is common of girl's friendships). Activities can include playing video games, sporting activities, watching movies or social drinking.

Origin

It is rumored a skateboard magazine coined the phrase in the 1990's, it referred to the relationships that develop between skaters who spent a great deal of time together.

"Pauly and Vin have such a bromance it's crazy"

See also **Man-crush, Homosocial**.

BRONX ZOO

Pronounced: (brahnks zoo)

Noun

A club with a lot of ugly girls in it.

"It's like a Bronx Zoo in here, we need to bounce."

See also **Hippopotamus**.

BUBBIES
Noun
Female breasts.
See also **Ta-Ta's, Bolt-Ons**.

BUSTED
Noun
An ugly unattractive female.
See also **Landmine, Grenade**

BURGERS FOR BOYS
Phrase
This phrase is used when it is time to eat. Whether cooking for yourself , ordering takeout or going to a restaurant.

The New Jersey Shore Dictionary

CABS ARE HERE!

Pronounced: (kabs r hear)
Phrase
Should be said multiple times before leaving for a club as soon as the cab arrives to take everyone to the club. Cabs are used to drive to the club due to the heavy drinking so they will not have to drive back from the club late at night.

CALAMAD

Pronounced: (kahlamahd)
Noun
Another word for calamari, the Italian name for squid, which is served fried at Italian restaurants.
"Pass me the frickin calamad!"

CAMEL TOE

Pronounced: (caml tow)
Noun
Refers to the outline of a female's labia majora seen through tight pants, underwear, swimwear.
"Jennie's got quite the camel toe showing!"

CAPER

Pronounced: (cay-purr)
Noun
An event of some sort, sometimes secret, sometimes not.
See also **Creep**

CHECKIN IN

Pronounced: (check-in in)
Phrase
Used to let someone know that you are around.
Usually used with a girlfriend when you call her to let her know you are available.
"Hi Samee, I am just checkin' in."

CHIA

Pronounced: (chee-ah)
Noun
A woman's pubic region.
"Her chia was clean and shaved."

CHINESE EYES

Pronounced: (Chi-nees ayes)
Noun
When someone is so drunk that they have to squint their eyes in order to see properly.
Also known as **Chi Eyes**.

CHUBBED UP
Pronounced: (chubd up)
Verb
To get an erection.
"The way you work that pole like a pro is getting me <u>*chubbed up.*</u>*"*

CHUCKY
Pronounced: (chukee)
Noun
A female vagina.
"Quit talkin about your puffy chucky."

COCK BLOCK
Pronounced: (kok blok)
Noun
To prevent a male friend or associate from getting some action. Or a situation that prevents someone from getting action or hooking up..
"Vito, you should have taken the grenade instead of trying to <u>*cock block*</u> *me."*

COOL DOWN
Pronounced: (kool daon)
Action
Before going to sleep in a hot non-air conditioned house you: a. Take a shower b. Put a wet wash cloth on your head c. Hope to fall asleep within 15 minutes before you are hot again and have to repeat process.

CRANKIN DOWN
Pronounced: (crayn-kin down)
Verb
Can be used in reference to having sex or can also be used in reference to quickly drink or eat something.
"I'd really like to <u>crank</u> her <u>down</u>."
"Damn Vin! You're really <u>crankin' down</u> those beers!"

CREEP
Pronounced: (kreep)
Verb
Hit on girls.
"Time to do some creepin at the club."

CRICKET
Pronounced: (crick-it)
Noun
Lower-class chick, typically one who a guy would hook up with for sex.
"Those girls at the club last night were solid <u>cricket</u>s."

CUNTY
Pronounced: (kun-tee)
Verb
Someone who is cunty is either a female that is being a bitch or a male that is acting like a female.
"Jane, why does your daughter have to be so <u>cunty</u>?"
Adjective
Describe someone as being the ultimate bitch.
"You are the <u>cuntiest</u> son of a bitch I've ever met."

DO THE RIGHT THING

Pronounced: (Do, th rite thng)
Phrase
To treat a girl right. Treating a girl with respect. Don't treat her like a one night stand.
"Do the right thing with wifey"
See also **Wifey.**

DTF

Pronounced: (dtf)
Noun, Adjective
This is an acronym for Down to Fuck. Means a girl is "ready to sleep with you" (a.k.a. have sex). Looked at as a sure thing.
"That girl is DTF" or *"I met this DTF girl at the club and took her back to my place last night"*
See also **DTS.**

DTS

Pronounced: (dts)
Noun, Adjective
This is an acronym for Down to Snuggle. Means a girl will sleep in your bed next to you but will not have sex with you.
"That girl is DTS but I'd rather her be DTF!"
"I met this DTS girl at the club and took her back to my place last night" See also **DTS.**

DIGITZ

Pronounced: (Dig-its)
Noun
This refers to a phone number.
See also **Gettin Numbers.**

DIRTY LITTLE HAMSTER

Pronounced: (Drtee Litl hamstir)
Noun
This refers to a girl who leaves dirty sanitary pads lying around in plain site.
"That girl is a dirty little hamster"

DOWN THE SHORE

Pronounced: (Down th shoor)
Noun
A synonym for New Jersey. Refers to the Atlantic coast of New Jersey and all adjacent motels, resorts and communities.
"See ya down the shore"

EASY BRO

Pronounced: (e-z bro)

Expression

Means take it easy.

"Hey now, I don't want to get in a scuffle here. Easy, bro!"

EIFFEL TOWER

Pronounced: (iful tahwr)

Noun

A threesome with two guys and a girl. The guys high-five over the girl to make the Eiffel tower shape.

"Hey Pauli, remember when we Eiffel towered Linda?"

ELEPHANT

Pronounced: (l-ifant)

Noun

An ugly large girl. Usually overweight and on the heavy side. A member of the Bronx Zoo and a Zoo Creature.

"Look at the size of that Elephant !"

See also **Bronx Zoo, Zoo Creature**.

FAKE TANS
Pronounced: (fak tans)
Noun
Any form of alcohol in cans, like beer. Also a reference to spray tanning.
"I am going to get drunk on the fake tans tonight."

FEEL YOU
Pronounced: (feel u)
Verb
To understand or sympathize with.
"Hey man, I feel you."

FETCH
Pronounced: (fe-chuh)
Adjective
Used to describe something cool and trendy.
"That outfit is so fetch."

FISHER PRICE
Pronounced: (fish-er pryce)
Verb
To explain something so an idiot will understand.
"Let me Fisher Price it for you… a grenade is an ugly girl."

FIST PUMP

Pronounced: (fist pump)
Proper Noun
The act of closing your hand into a fist and waving it up and down to the beat of the music in the club. The action gets faster and faster as the music increases.

How To
Step A: Clench (Close) your fist, retract the forearm towards the shoulder in a hammer fashion.

Step B: Extend the fist outward to the side of one's body until desired length is reached (start with short lengths and increase as music plays)

Step C: Repeat.
"The <u>fist pump</u> by the group was astounding."

FLAPPED

Pronounced: (flapt)
Verb
To get overly excited.
"I'm getting all <u>flapped</u> about the girls coming by today."

FRED FLINTSTONE TOE

Pronounced: (fred flynston tow)
Noun
An ugly woman's big toe.

FRESH TO DEATH - FTD

Pronounced: (fre shhh too Deth)
Verb
To have the trendiest and hottest items out there. Also refers to being in style with the latest items.

FUGAZI

Pronounced: (fug ahh z)
Noun
A fake or false item. Relates to knock-offs of popular designer clothes, jewelry, purses etc.
"Where did you get that purse, you know it's a fugazi right?"

FUGLY

Pronounced: (fug lee)
Adjective
Fucking ugly.
"Bro, she looks fugly."
See also **Grenade**.

FULL HOT

Pronounced: (fool hawt)
Adjective
The state of being fully angry or fully chubbed up over a particular matter or situation.
"Vito was full hot when Angelina was in the club talking smack about him."
See also **Chubbed Up, Half Hot, Hot**.

GETTIN NUMBERS

Pronounced: (getn brz)
Phrase
Getting girls phone numbers at the club.
"Wow we sure were gettin numbers tonight at the club!"

GOING TO TOWN

Pronounced: (go-ing too town)
Phrase
Meaning no holds barred. Get down and dirty with whatever you are doing. Usually in reference to two girls going down on each other.
"I want both you girls just to go to town on each other."

GOT HEAT

Pronounced: (gawt heet)
Phrase
Said when someone is angry at you or you're angry at someone else.
"Pauli's got heat with me after I accused him of talking smack"

GOO

Pronounced: (goooo)
Phrase
Italian American food.
"I'd much rather have Moms Itialian cooking than this goo."

GORILLA

Pronounced: (go ril a)
Noun
A male guido that is very large and muscular. Likes to show off his chest. Popular with guidettes.
"Jessie, check out that gorilla over by the waiter"
See also **Guido, Guidette**.

GORILLA CENTRAL

Pronounced: (go ril a sentrl)
Noun
An establishment with an abundance of gorilla's.
"That club was like gorilla central last night!"
See also **Gorilla**.

GFA

Pronounced: (gfa)
Noun
Acronym for Grenade Free America. Relates to wanting to see just beautiful woman all the time.
"Why can't this country be GFA?"
See also **Grenade** .

GREASED

Pronounced: (greesed)
Adjective
Used to describe how dirty something is.
"I stayed in this motel room over the summer that had the worst, greased up, piece of shit bathroom I'd ever seen."

GREASE MONKEY

Pronounced: (greese munkee)
Noun
Nicely tanned Italian that's good with cars.

GRENADE

Pronounced: (gra naad)
Noun
An ugly girl or group of girls if plural. Usually found at clubs after midnight. The solitary ugly girl always found with a group of hotties. If the grenade doesn't get any action, then neither does anyone else. (see cock blocker) A grenade is not always a hippo but is always busted.
Use
Someone in your group of friends will sacrifice himself by hooking up with the grenade in order for the guy(s) to have a chance of having sex with the hot girl(s).
"Pauli, check out the grenades in this club, looks like it's time to bounce."
See also **Busted, GTL, Trenade.**

GRENADE LAUNCHER

Pronounced: (gra nad lawnchr)
Noun
A bigger version of the grenade.
"Did you see that fugly grenade launcher on the dance floor?"
See also **Hippopotamus**.

GRENADE JUMPER

Pronounced: (gra nad jmpr)
Noun
A guy who will be with the grenade so that his friend will have a chance to hook up with the hot girl. Most of the time the grenade jumper will get laid and the friend with the hottie ends up with nothing.
"Hey Vito, Can you be a grenade jumper tonight?"

GRINDING

Pronounced: (grine ding)
Verb
Dancing with a partner in a close sexual manner. Genital regions will make contact with clothing.

GTL

Pronounced: (gtl)
Noun
An acronym for the combination of three words – Gym, Tan, Laundry. Describes the act of doing all three on a daily basis.

GTL (CONT)

Also known to stand for Grenade, Tank, Landmine.
"Wake up guys it's time to GTL."
"This place is full of GTL's, let's bounce."
See also **Gym, Tan, Laundry, Fresh to Death, Grenade, Tank, Landmine**.

GUIDO

Pronounced: (gweedo)
Noun, Adjective
An Italian American man residing in New York or New Jersey but is also found in other areas around the world.

Some Italians self-identify as "guidos", the term is often considered derogatory or an ethnic slur.

Style
Clothing associated with the term includes gold chains (often cornicellos, figaro chains, herringbone chains, or saint medallions), pinky rings, plain T-shirts, muscle shirts, leather jackets, sweat suits, unbuttoned (top 3 buttons) dress shirts and dress suits. The guido will also spend large amounts of time looking at themselves in mirrors.

Often attracted to the female version of himself, the guidette..
"Look at that guy, he is such a guido."
See also **Guidette**.

GUIDETTE

Pronounced: (gweedet)
Noun, Adjective
An Italian American woman residing in New York or New Jersey but is also found in other areas around the world. The female counterpart to the "Guido".

Style
A Guidette can be recognized by her tanning and either very light or very dark hair. Guidette's have an overly sexual demeanor. A Guidette will spend an excessive amount of time on her appearance, makeup and looking at themselves in mirrors.

Often attracted to the male version of herself, the guido..
"Look at that girl, she is such a guidette.."
See also **Guido**.

GYM

Pronounced: (jim)
Proper Noun
This is one of the daily tasks of a guido. Usually performed in the mornings before tanning and laundry. Word is mostly used as an acronym GTL.
"Wake up time to hit the gym!"
See also **GTL, Tanning, Laundry** .

HALF HOT

Pronounced: (haf hawt)

Adjective

The state of being half angry or half chubbed up over a particular matter or situation.

"Johnnie got half hot when Samee screamed at him'."

See also **Chubbed Up, Hot, Full Hot**.

HANGER ON-ER

Pronounced: (hayng-er on-er)

Noun

A girl who gets easily attached to a guy.

"I banged this groupie last night, and I sort of regret it. She won't stop calling me, I think I've got a hanger on-er."

See also **Stage Five Clinger**.

HATERADE

Pronounced: (haytr aid)

Noun

A fictional beverage, parodying a popular sports drink, consumed by individuals who are jealous of others, supposedly fueling their ability to be jealous of, or hate on others.

"I just served up a big glass of haterade on that fool."

HELL OF A HAND

Pronounced: (hell-uh-vah haynd)
Phrase
To have something great on your side.
"He had 2 strippers making out in his lap while receiving a lap dance from both last night. He got dealt a hell of a hand."

HIPPOPOTAMUS

Pronounced: (hip o pot a muss)
Noun
The ugly looking girlfriend. Also can be referred to as a grenade and are always busted. Usually overweight and on the heavy side. A member of the Bronx Zoo.
"Look at the size of that Hippopotamus with that chick!"
See also **Bronx Zoo, Busted, Grenade**.

HOMOSOCIAL

Pronounced: (hawt)
Noun
Describes same-sex relationships that are not of a romantic or sexual nature, such as friendship, mentorship, or others.
"Boy Vin and Vito seem awful close, you might think they are homosocial."
See also **Bromance**.

HOT

Pronounced: (hawt)

Adjective

When a something is awesome or when a female is pretty.

"You should've seen Vito last night after that jabroni said that Samee is hot."

Verb

To be very angry and someone or something.

"You should've seen Vito last night after that jabroni dropped off Samee, he was so hot that she was late."

See also **Bangin, Half Hot, Full Hot**.

HOT FREAKS

Pronounced: (hawt freeks)

Noun

Usually 2 strippers who are lesbians. Can be used for anything hot where girls are getting freaky.

"You're lapping her like a dog drinking for a water bowl on a hot summer day. You are one hot freak."

HOTTEST EVER

Pronounced: (hawt-est ev-er)

Phrase

When a girl is extremely beautiful.

"Jennie is the hottest ever!"

HYENA

Pronounced: (hi eena)

Noun

A sexually aggressive young girl who preys on older men.

IFF
Pronounced: (iff)
Noun
An acronym for the I'm Fucked Foundation. A term which means you have been caught and are in trouble with your girlfriend. Johnnie is usually seen here.
"Bro, Samee found out and now I am in the IFF"

IF YOU HAVE TO THINK ABOUT IT – IT IS
Pronounced: (i-m just say-in)
Phrase
Said when referencing a guy dressed as a girl. Basically it is a dude. Relates to Vito when he scammed on a trenade.
"Vito, If you have to think about it – it is!."
See also **Trenade**.

IGGY
Pronounced: (ig-ee)
Noun
Inside tidbit of information. Here's the iggy on the Jen situation would mean here's the inside dirt on Jen.
"What's the inside iggy Samee?"
Also known as **Inside Iggy**.

IN THAT CAPACITY

Pronounced: (in that k-pass-itee)
Adjective
Describes the extent of a particular subject matter.

JABRONI

Pronounced: (juh-bro-nee)
Noun, Adjective
Loser, chump or to do something stupid.
Adjective
"First jabroni move, he didn't open the car door for Jennie."
Noun
"What a jabroni, he didn't open the car door for Jennie."
Can also be used as **Jabrone** *(Pronounced: juh-brone)*

JERSEY PLATE

Pronounced: (gerzee pleight)
Noun
A tramp stamp. Tattoo on the back just above the butt – lower back tattoo. Mostly done by females.

JERSEY RIDER

Pronounced: (gerzee rydr)
Noun
A woman who dates an athlete for status. Similar to a gold digger.

JERSEY SALUTE

Pronounced: (gerzee saloot)
Verb
Use of the middle finger.

JERSEY SHORE STAND

Pronounced: (gerzee shoar stnd)

Noun

A one-night stand where there is a 99% chance of seeing that person again.

JERSEY SHOWER

Pronounced: (gerzee shawr)

Noun

When you don't want to take an shower and you spray cologne/perfume all over yourself so no one can smell your body odor.

JERSEY SHUFFLE

Pronounced: (gerzee shufel)

Noun

When driving you cross more than 3 lanes of traffic in a vehicle without pausing or using a turn signal, usually to get to an exit.

Also known as the jersey slide or jersey swerve when crossing a single lane without a turn signal.

JUICEHEADS

Pronounced: (joos hedz)

Noun, Adjective

A person who uses steroids in order to aid in the production of muscle mass. Usually hunted by guidettes.

Noun

"What a juicehead, he didn't open the car door for Jennie."

KOOKA

Pronounced: (koo-kah)
Noun
A term for the anus.
Noun
"I saw her Kooka."

KICK'EM OUT WIDE

Pronounced: (kik-em owt wyde)
Expression
Term means to give it your all. Also a reference to a girl opening her legs wide in bed.
"I popped a few beers last night and I was ready to <u>kick'em out wide</u>!"

"As soon as I got home, my girl hopped on the bed and <u>kicked'em out wide</u>… it was a dream come true!"

LANDMINE

Pronounced: (land myn)

Noun

A thin ugly girl or if plural a group of thin girls.
"Bro, there's too many landmines on the dance floor, I barely made it over here alive."
See also **Grenade, Tank**.

LAUNDRY

Pronounced: (lawn-dree)

Verb

Used to describe the act of going to a Laundromat to wash clothes so they can be fresh for going to the club. The third part of the GTL daily routine.
"Bro, lets go laundry up."
See also **GTL, Gym, Tanning**.

LEAVE HER ASIDE

Pronounced: (Leev Her Asyd)

Phrase

When a friend asks you not to touch or talk to a certain girl. You should respect him and not try to hit on the girl while your friend isn't around. This also applies to calling or texting her.
"Leave her aside Vito, I really like her, this could turn into something long term.""

LINCOLN LOG

Pronounced: (link-in lawg)

Noun

A turd or a piece of poop.

"Holy crap, you should've seen the size of the Lincoln log I laid last night."

LOCAL

Pronounced: (low kul)

Noun

Someone who is from New Jersey and lives at the Jersey Shore all year round.

LOVER

Pronounced: (luvr)

Noun

Someone who is a signifigant other, usually only used for sex.

"Do you have a boyfriend or a husband or just a lover?"

MAD WORK

Pronounced: (mad wurk)
Verb
The act of doing crazy stuff.
"Johnnie is doing some mad work on those 3 chicks."

MAN CRUSH

Pronounced: (mayn cru shh)
Noun
A close but non-sexual relationship between two (or more) men.
"Pauli and Vin have a man crush."
See also **Bromance**.

MAN UP

Pronounced: (mayn Up)
Verb
Be a man and tell it like it is, even if the truth hurts.
"Why don't you man up and tell it like it is instead of being a pussy and saying nothing?"

MANATEE FLIPPER ARMS
Pronounced: (man-a-tee flip-purr ahrms)
Noun
Someone that has really fat lunch lady arms.

MANIPULATE THE SITUATION
Pronounced: (mayn-ip-yoo-layt tha sitch-yoo-ay-shun)
Phrase
When someone tries to get someone to do something that would make for a great time.
"Bro, I'm trying to manipulate the situation here."
See also **Situation.**

MOSQUITO
Pronounced: (mas kee tow)
Expression
Sometimes referred to as Jersey mosquito, unusually large mosquitoes which are called crane flies.

MVP
Pronounced: (mvp)
Noun
Most Valuable Player
"MVP, MVP, MVP!."
"Wow, check it out, it's MVP"
See also **Markin' Out.**

MARKIN' OUT

Pronounced: (mahrk-in owt)
Verb
The act of being a super fan.
"OK, I think I'm done markin' out to MVP."
See also **MVP**.

MILK DISPENSERS

Pronounced: (milk dis-spen-sirs)
Noun
A woman's breasts.
"Whoa, check out those milk dispensers on that hottie."
See also **Bolt-Ons** and **Ta-Ta's**.

MY BOY

Pronounced: (my boy)
Expression
A best friend who is male.
"Who's that in the jacuzzi? Oh, it's my boy, Vin."

NGZ

Pronounced: (ngz)
Proper Noun
Acronym for No Grenade Zone. Means all girls around are beautiful and there are no ugly girls in site. A rare club occurrence.

ON THE BACKSIDE
Pronounced: (on the back-side)
Noun
Something that will be done later or in addition to.
"OK, let's hit the tanning then <u>on the backside</u> we'll get the laundry."

POUF
Pronounced: (poof)
Noun
A female blown up or enlarged piece of hair that is held in place with a lot of hairspray and a banana clip.
"Your pouf is looking hot tonight Jessie!" - *Vin*
See also **Snook Look**.

POUND
Pronounced: (pownd)
Verb
To have aggressive sex.
Verb
To drink heavily.
Noun
Form of greeting where two fists meet at the knuckles.
"I want to pound every girl in Seaside!"
See also **Cabs are Here**, **Smush**.

PROSTITUTION WHORE
Pronounced: (prastushun hoar)
Noun
Someone who has been engaged many times over.
See also **Jersey Shore Stand**.

PLAY YOU OUT

Pronounced: (pla u awt)
Phrase
The act of being done wrong by a friend.
"I am going to play him out."

PUNKED

Pronounced: (punkd)
Verb
To be disrespected.
See also **Play You Out.**

PUSSIFICATION

Pronounced: (puss if ikashun)
Noun, Verb
The act of being a pussy.
"Look at that guy in the passenger seat, having his woman drive him around. That kind of crap is leading to the Pussification of America."

PUT IT OVER

Pronounced: (put it o-ver)
Phrase
The act of glorifying something or making a case for something so everyone has the same stance on this issue as you do.
"I think kicking Angelina out is the best solution, I'm gonna keep saying it until I put it over."

QUITE NICELY

Pronounced: (kwite nighslee)
Phrase
To be real nice.
"Vito made a move on that girl quite nicely."

READY TO GO
Pronounced: (reddi to gao)
Verb
Act of being upset.
"Screw that jerk, I am ready to go."

RICED OUT
Pronounced: (r-eyesd awt)
Adjective
Someone who makes unnecessary modifications to their car to make it look like the car will go fast (mostly Asian import cars hence the original term rice). Includes imports and exports usually cars that are small, slow, cheap, and designed to go slow. Parts used are neon lights, loud exhausts, over the top spoilers and lots of stickers.

RIDER
Pronounced: (rydur)
Noun
A car that has turned into a rust bucket originating from the Jersey salted roads during the winter.
"Bro, That guy just bought a $25,000 new car, In 3 years of winter driving that car's gonna be such a jersey rider!"

RIGID

Pronounced: (rij-id)
Verb

To be real rough around the edges. Solid.

"Most truckers are real <u>rigid</u> men, but everyone once in a while you get a few female truckers, but they're <u>rigid</u> also, for the most part."

ROBBERY

Pronounced: (roburee)
Verb

When a best friend tries to steal your girlfriend.

"Vito tried a <u>robbery</u> on Vin's chick"

See also **Cock Blocker**.

RUGGED

Pronounced: (rug-gid)
Verb

To be very manly.

"Quit roughin' me up you big <u>rugged</u> 250 pound man."

See also **Block Rocker**.

SAMEECH
Pronounced: (sam itch)
Verb
A type of sandwich made with only the very best ingredients, with connotations of extra goodness. Only the very best meats, cheeses, veggies, condiments.
"Make me a Sameech, I am starving."

SHIT STIRRER
Pronounced: (shit sturr-er)
Noun
A person who agitates a situation between two other people in order to get them to fight each other, as things begin to escalate the person disappears.
"Vito was being a shit stirrer between Johnnie and Samee."

SITUATION
Pronounced: (sitchuashun)
Noun
Denotes the expected arrival of reasonably attractive girls for an informal social gathering.
"Oh shit, we have a situation."
Also refers to well defined six pack abs.
"Check out this situation."

SLASH
Pronounced: (slash)
Verb
Used when there is more than one word for something.
"Jennie is a business owner slash model."

SMURF
Pronounced: (cmrf)
Noun
Cute short little girl.
"Look at the cute little smurf."
See also **Snook Look**.

SMUSH OR SMOOSH
Pronounced: (cmush/cmoosh)
Noun
Have sex.
"I'd love to smush her." "Lets smoosh"
See also **Pound**.

SNOOK LOOK
Pronounced: (snok luhk)
Noun
When a girl wears tight leopard dress with high heels and has her hair in a pouf.
"Hey, I love that Snook Look, let's go smush."
See also **Pouf, Smush**.

SOLID

Pronounced: (sawlid)
Adjective, Exclamation
Term meaning awesone.
"Solid!"

SOLID GOLD

Pronounced: (sawlid goald)
Noun
When something is the best or a classic.
"That girl is solid gold."

SPIN MOVE

Pronounced: (spin moov)
Noun
Spin around and out of the way when you are near a girl where she doesn't notice you are gone.
"I pulled a spin move on her to get away from that grenade"

STAGE FIVE CLINGER

Pronounced: (staguh 5 klingr)
Noun
Member of the opposite sex who is overly attached early on in a relationhip.
"Vanessa's becoming a stage five clinger, I have to dump her before she turns into a stalker."

STIFF

Pronounced: (stiff)
Verb
To be real lame and plain. No fun.
"Those girls last night were so stiff they didn't get naked."

STOOGE

Pronounced: (stewj)
Noun
Someone who is a clown or a goof.

SUCK OFF

Pronounced: (suk off)
Verb
To give head.
"How many guys would you say you sucked off?."

SUNROOF

Pronounced: (sunruuf)
Verb
A visor. Only acceptable when worn by football coaches, tailgaters, or beach-goer's.

SWERVE

Pronounced: (Swerv)
Verb
To lead someone in the wrong direction.
"He tried to swerve me ongoing back to his place but I didn't fall for it."

TAKING ONE FOR THE TEAM

Pronounced: (taakng won for the teem)
Phrase
Spending time with a grenade, tank or landmine so your bro can get together with a hottie.
"Vito, Can't you take one for the team and hook up with the grenade for tonight?"
See also **Bro, Grenade, Landmine, Tank**.

TA-TA'S

Pronounced: (Tah-Tah's)
Noun
A woman's breasts.
"Those were a nice pair of ta-ta's on her."
See also **Milk Dispensers**, **Bolt-Ons**.

TANK

Pronounced: (tanx)
Noun
A large ugly woman.
"I couldn't get by the tank on the way over here."
See also **Grenade, Landmine**.

TANNING

Pronounced: (tan-ing)
Verb
Done on a daily basis, action requires going to a tanning salon and using a tanning bed. Also could be done by going to the beach and laying in the sunshine for a specified amount of time. The time varies bases on the skin tone of the guido or guidette.

The second part to the GTL daily routine.
"Let's head to the beach and get some <u>tanning</u> done before we hit the club tonight."
See also **GTL, Gym, Laundry**

THICK

Pronounced: (thik)
Verb
To be very muscled.
"With a little work, Vin can be one <u>thick</u> mother fucker."

THICK AS THIEVES

Pronounced: (thik az theevs)
Adjective
The bond between Italian families and friends.
"As a family, we are <u>thick as thieves</u>. We will always be there for each other and protect each other."

TORPEDO

Pronounced: (tra nayd)

Noun

A car that Guido's drive.

Types

1. A domestic car that has been riced out (ie: 90' Mustang with large chrome wheels, body kit, loud exhaust, and large rear spoiler)
2. An import car with muscle car accessories (ie: Accord painted red with black racing stripes, large rear tires, cowl inducted hood scoop, and side pipes. Sometimes painted with yellow flames).

Vin: What the hell is making that sound?
Pauli: Fuckin guido torpedo just drove by.

See also **Riced Out**

TRENADE

Pronounced: (tra nayd)

Noun

An ugly guy dressed as a girl. An ugly transvestite/tranny.

"Didn't you see the adams apple ? Are you kidding me, that girl was a trenade all the way!

T-SHIRT TIME

Pronounced: (tee shrt tym)

Phrase, Noun

A ritual to put on a freshly laundered t-shirt. Usually follows tank top time which is done before going to a club.

UNDER THE GUISE

Pronounced: (un-durr tha guys)
Verb
To be undercover or disguised.
"So I had the idea to sell my own urine, under the guise of beer."

VIBE
Pronounced: (vib)
Verb
To be attracted to someone.
"I am vibin on that hot chick over there."
See also **Creep**.

WAAAAAAH
Pronounced: (waaaah)
Adjective
Loud sound of disappointment.

WAR OUT THERE
Pronounced: (war awt thair)
Phrase
When there is a lot of grenades, tanks and landmines at a club. Too many ugly girls in one place at one time.
"Vin, do you see what's going on here ? There's a war out there in this club."
See also **Bronx Zoo**.

WIFEY
Pronounced: (wi fee)
Noun
A girl you can bring home to your mother. A girl you could marry.
"Pauli. I think I see my future wifey."
See also **Wife Up**.

WIFE UP

Pronounced: (wif up)

Adjective

Be with a girl in a serious relationship that could lead to marriage.

"Pauli. I am going to wife up that girl."

See also **Wifey**.

WINGMAN

Pronounced: (wing mahn)

Noun

A partner in crime, a true friend. A person who will always have your back, no matter what. He or she will save you.

Action

Someone who goes along with their friend on a date so that when their friend picks up the hot girl the wingman gets stuck with her ugly friend. Guys usually switch off wingmen at different clubs.

The Wingman will always be there to occupy time with the least attractive girl of the pair so that you may engage in conversation with the hottie.

Often, when an attractive girl is out with an ugly friend, she often feels restricted to not leave that ugly friend alone, thus making the hot girl, un-touchable.

When the wingman technique is used, both girls are approached by the men, and the Wingman

WINGMAN (CONT)

automatically engages in conversation with the ugly girl and jumps on the grenade.
"Hey Vito, Be my wingman at the club tonight so I can get some action with a hottie!"

WORK OUT
Pronounced: (werk awt)
Phrase
Going to the gym for a particular workout.

Action
Start with bench presses (Usually 3 reps every set)

Next bicep curls with dumbbells.

This allows concentration on chest and partial arms rather than triceps, back, abdominals, and most importantly, legs and cardio.
"I walked into the gym and heard screams of agony. The guido's must be maxing out their bench presses again."

WORKED INTO A FRENZY
Pronounced: (werk-ed in-too a fren-zee)
Phrase
The act of getting worked up over a particular subject matter.
"Don't get worked into a frenzy over the girl."

WOUNDED SOLDIER

Pronounced: (wunded souljer)
Phrase
Any beer at a club or party that has been abandoned by it's original owner.
"Jenni drank all the <u>wounded soldiers</u> at the party."

XRAPE

Pronounced: (ex raap)
Noun
The act of undressing a person with one's eyes while simultaneously imagining oneself involved in sexual activity with that person.

XRATED

Pronounced: (ex raatd)
Adjective
Lewd or obscene.
"That girl on the stripper pole is xrated."

YOU RE THE MAN

Pronounced: (your tha mayn)
Phrase

Means how it sounds.

THE NEW
JERSEY SHORE
Dictionary

ZINGER
Pronounced: (zing-er)
Noun
A diss or good come back.
"Ooooh, whatta zinger!"

ZOO CREATURE
Pronounced: (zing-er)
Noun
In the family of the hippopotamus or elephant.
See also , **Bronx Zoo, Hippopotamus**.

INDEX

Made in the USA
Lexington, KY
31 March 2012